Dedicated to Katie Lindblom.
For all those big anxieties
in such a short little person.
I loved you then,
I love you now!

I0163466

Deep in the woods, just past your neighborhood...

Further yet down from the stream, living inside that big oak tree...

Thrives a tiny little colony.

They have fuzz of black and yellow...

And fragile little wings.

They buzz around looking for pollen and other sweet things...

hello!

And no one's afraid to go up to a flower and say "Hello!"

That is, except for one tiny little bee who always thinks "Oh, No!"

oh no!

When it comes to any kind of social swarm, her instincts are:

Fight,

Flight,

And flee.

She often finds herself wrapped
up in her worry,

And at times being a little bit
too negative and fidgety

These things can make it
hard for our anxious bee to
fully fly.

So how can we make it
better? Or how can we try?

1. Identi-fly

Identify what makes you stressed
out and ask yourself why.

2. Talk to the hive

In order to thrive, sometimes you need to talk with the rest of your hive.

3. Stop to smell the flowers

Sometimes we need to take a deep breath and focus on the things that make us happy and calm. What are some things that help you after your April Showers?

4. What are your "Buzz Words"?

Think of words you can use to express how you feel in those moments so you are more prepared for next time.

5. Know when your colony is under attack and when to ask for a helping hand.

Sometimes, like in our friend's case, she'll need therapy to help her understand and on a solution safely land.

Whether you are a girl or a bumble-boy, It's important to find what brings you joy.

And always remember:

Just because you feel stress,
doesn't make you any less.

You can still be
funny,

Still make - and
enjoy! - honey.

You are still you, even when this book is through.

The author:

A grad student of the University of Strathclyde for Library and Information Science in Glasgow, United Kingdom, Jaz is a 24-year-old who loves books and bringing culture, education, and emotional literacy to children and adults in creative ways. Jaz believes that every emotion is valid and should be heard as much as the person feeling it needs it to be. Her favorite animal is a raccoon, which gives inspiration for her other writing.

The illustrator:

A budding artist from New Jersey, Alyssa creates to combat the daily darknesses of life. She firmly believes in the bright side of every situation and is determined to share her vision of all things cute and sweet with anyone who will lend an eye. Having graduated with a BFA in illustration, Alyssa aims to use her skills to spread positivity and emotional support whenever she can. She is a lover of all animals - but especially cats - and is perhaps overly-fond of the color pink.

If you enjoyed our book and would like to see future publishings - including free storytime on our blog! - please visit www.callofthechildbooks.com or visit us on Facebook at Call Of The Child Books.

www.ingramcontent.com/pod-product-compliance
Lightning Source LLC
Chambersburg PA
CBHW040230070426

42448CB00035B/286